Thomas Edison

INVENTOR,
SCIENTIST,
and GENIUS

by **LORI MORTENSEN**
illustrated by **JEFFREY THOMPSON**

PICTURE WINDOW BOOKS
Minneapolis, Minnesota

Special thanks to our advisers for their expertise:

Louis Carlat, Ph.D.
Thomas A. Edison Papers
Rutgers, The State University of New Jersey

Susan Kesselring, M.A., Literacy Educator
Rosemount–Apple Valley–Eagan (Minnesota) School District

Editor: Nick Healy
Designer: Nathan Gassman
Page Production: Melissa Kes
Associate Managing Editor: Christianne Jones
The illustrations in this book were created digitally.
Photo Credit: Library of Congress, page 3

Picture Window Books
5115 Excelsior Boulevard, Suite 232
Minneapolis, MN 55416
877-845-8392
www.picturewindowbooks.com

Printed in the United States of America.

Library of Congress Cataloging-in-Publication Data
Mortensen, Lori, 1955-
Thomas Edison : inventor, scientist, and genius / by Lori Mortensen ; illustrated by
Jeffrey Thompson.
p. cm.
Includes bibliographical references and index.
ISBN-13: 978-1-4048-3105-6 (library binding)
ISBN-10: 1-4048-3105-3 (library binding)
ISBN-13: 978-1-4048-3484-2 (paperback)
ISBN-10: 1-4048-3484-2 (paperback)
1. Edison, Thomas A. (Thomas Alva), 1847-1931—Juvenile literature.
2. Inventors—United States—Biography—Juvenile literature.
3. Electric engineers—United States—Biography—Juvenile literature.
I. Thompson, Jeffrey (Jeffrey Allen), 1970- II. Title.
TK140.E3M69 2006
621.3092—dc22
[B]   2006027227

Thomas Edison was a great inventor. He was most famous for making a safe electric lightbulb. His other inventions made it possible for people to see moving pictures, brought music into homes, and much more. Thomas changed the world by improving the way people lived.

This is the story of Thomas Edison.

Thomas Alva Edison was born in 1847. His family lived in a small Ohio town called Milan. Everyone called him Al. Even at a young age, he was always asking questions.

One day, he asked his mother why hens sat on eggs. She told him hens kept eggs warm so chicks would hatch. Hours later, the boy's family found him sitting on a big nest of broken eggs.

When Thomas was 6 years old, one of his experiments started the family's barn on fire. The building burned to the ground. If the fire had spread, it could have destroyed the town.

Thomas' father was very angry with him. Thomas would never forget the fire or the trouble it caused. Still, he did not stop trying to find answers to his questions.

As a boy, Thomas was often sick. His mother taught him at home because he missed so much school. Through his reading, Thomas learned how to make a laboratory and how to experiment with chemicals. He decided to set up his own lab in the basement.

From then on, he spent most of his time experimenting in his lab.

Thomas had to earn money to buy supplies for his experiments. When he was 12, he sold candy and newspapers on a train. He also printed his own newspaper, the *Weekly Herald*.

Later, Thomas lived in Newark, New Jersey. He married Mary Stilwell there on Christmas Day in 1871. But even a new wife could not keep him from thinking about inventions. After the wedding lunch, Thomas got an idea and rushed home to work on it.

In 1876, he opened a new lab in Menlo Park, New Jersey. The lab was one of the finest in the country. He hired a staff to help with his work. Thomas was one of the first people to make a living as an inventor.

Thomas got many ideas by trying to improve something else. One machine Thomas tried to improve was the telephone. In 1877, Thomas wanted to invent a way to save phone messages.

Instead, Thomas invented the phonograph. When the machine played back a nursery rhyme he read out loud, Thomas and his assistant were amazed. No one had ever heard a recorded voice before.

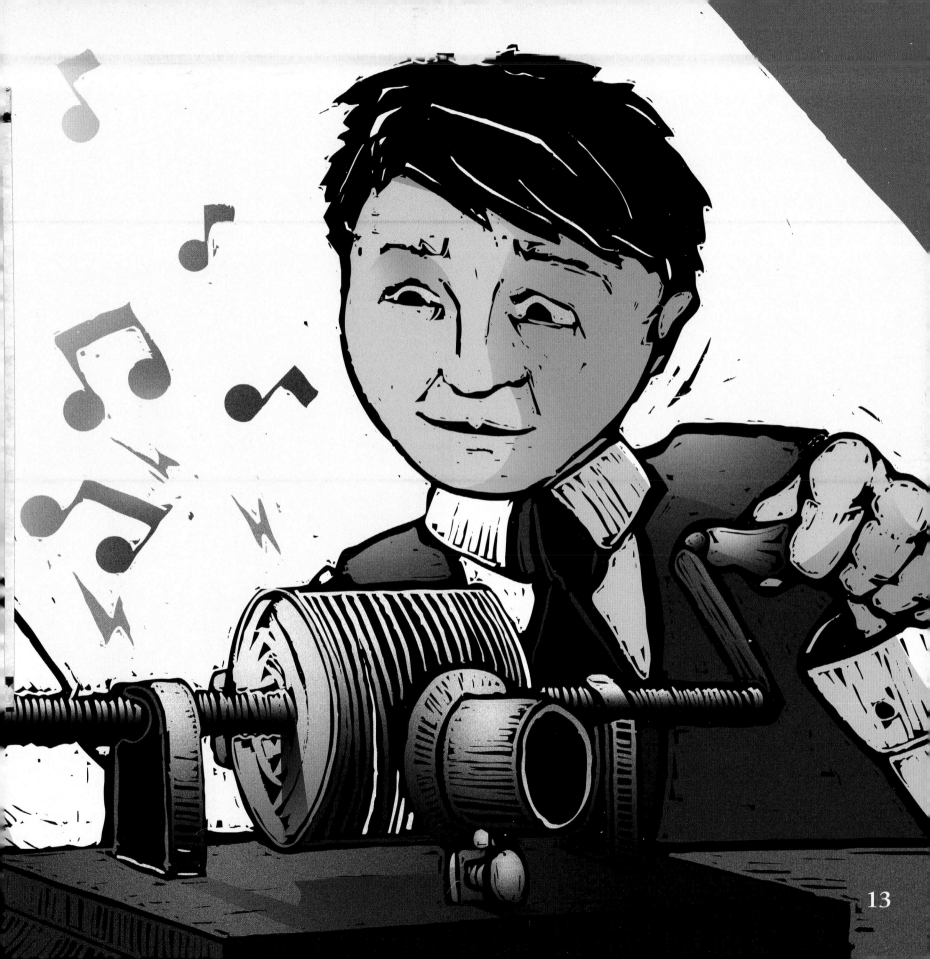

Soon Thomas went to work on making an electric lightbulb. At the time, most people used gaslights in their homes. Gaslights were dim and dangerous.

Other people had made lightbulbs before. However, the bulbs were unsafe. At worst, these early bulbs could start fires.

Thomas invented safe electric bulbs. He also worked on ways to safely supply electric power to businesses and homes.

On New Year's Eve 1879, Thomas invited everyone to see his new lightbulbs. Thousands of people came by wagon, train, and horseback. When Thomas' bulbs lit up the night, everyone cheered.

In time, electric bulbs would take the place of gaslights across the country.

Later, Thomas invented the first motion picture machine. He called it a kinetoscope. People dropped a nickel in a slot, turned a handle, and looked through a viewer. Then, like magic, they saw horses gallop and circus bears dance on film. Some early films simply showed Thomas' workers sneezing!

Thomas also invented a talking doll, a car battery, and portland cement. His cement was used to make Yankee Stadium, a famous ballpark in New York City.

Thomas Edison died in 1931 at the age of 84. By then, he had more than 1,000 patents for things he had invented. His inventions are still in use today.

At 10 p.m. on the night of Thomas' funeral, Americans turned off their lights for one minute to honor the great inventor.

The Life of Thomas Edison

1847	Born on February 11 in Milan, Ohio
1853	Burned down the family barn
1859	Sold candy and newspapers on the Grand Trunk Railroad
1871	Married Mary Stilwell
1876	Opened research laboratory in Menlo Park, New Jersey
1877	Invented the phonograph
1879	Demonstrated the electric lightbulb at Menlo Park laboratory
1884	Widowed when first wife died
1886	Married second wife, Mina Miller
1931	Died on October 18 in West Orange, New Jersey, at age 84

Did You Know?

Thomas was the youngest of seven children, but he grew up more like an only child. Three children died young. The other three were teenagers by the time he was born.

Thomas lost most of his hearing by the time he was 12 years old. Experts believe this was the result of childhood illnesses.

Thomas married twice and had three children with each wife.

Thomas' phonograph was so amazing that President Rutherford B. Hayes asked for a special demonstration at the White House. The first family stayed up until 3:30 a.m. playing with it.

Thomas is known for many sayings about success and failure, such as "I have not failed. I've just found 10,000 ways that won't work." And, "Genius is 1 percent inspiration, 99 percent perspiration."

GLOSSARY

chemical — a substance made by or used in chemistry, which is the study of substances, what they are made of, and what happens when they are mixed

experiment — a scientific way of testing or exploring an idea

genius — a person who has a great ability to think or a great talent

inventor — a person who makes or thinks of something for the first time

laboratory — a room used for experiments

patent — a paper from the government that allows the inventor to be the only person to make or sell an invention for a certain length of time

To Learn More

At the Library

Dooling, Michael. *Young Thomas Edison.* New York: Holiday House, 2005.

Editors at Time for Kids. *Thomas Edison: A Brilliant Inventor.* New York: Harper Trophy, 2005.

Raatma, Lucia. *Thomas Edison.* Minneapolis: Compass Point Books, 2004.

Schaefer, Lola M. *Thomas Edison.* Mankato, Minn.: Pebble Books, 2003.

On the Web

FactHound offers a safe, fun way to find Web sites related to this book. All of the sites on FactHound have been researched by our staff.

1. Visit *www.facthound.com*

2. Type in this special code: 1404831053

3. Click on the FETCH IT button.

Your trusty FactHound will fetch the best sites for you!

24

Index

Look for all of the books in the Biographies series:

Abraham Lincoln: Lawyer, President, Emancipator

Benjamin Franklin: Writer, Inventor, Statesman

Frederick Douglass: Writer, Speaker, and Opponent of Slavery

George Washington: Farmer, Soldier, President

Harriet Tubman: Hero of the Underground Railroad

Martin Luther King Jr.: Preacher, Freedom Fighter, Peacemaker

Pocahontas: Peacemaker and Friend to the Colonists

Sally Ride: Astronaut, Scientist, Teacher

Susan B. Anthony: Fighter for Freedom and Equality

Thomas Edison: Inventor, Scientist, and Genius